"*Jesus, the I AM* is an encouraging devotional designed for the forty days of Lent.

Written by the authors in an eight-sectioned fashion, it is relevant, insightful, and interesting. Invest time in this Jesus-centered and Jesus-saturated book and your life will be blessed, your heart encouraged, and your walk with the great I AM made sweeter."

—Dr. Randy Davis, executive director-treasurer,
Tennessee Baptist Mission Board

JESUS, THE
I AM
A DEVOTION FOR LENT

MARGIE WILLIAMSON
AND BENJIE SHAW

Birmingham, Alabama

Life Bible Study
An imprint of Iron Stream Media
100 Missionary Ridge
Birmingham, AL 35242
IronStreamMedia.com

Iron Stream Media serves its authors as they express their views, which may not express the views of the publisher.

Library of Congress Control Number: 2021947857

978-1-63204-124-1
978-1-63204-118-0 (ebook)

1 2 3 4 5—26 25 24 23 22

Contents

Preface..vii
Introduction..ix

Section 1: God Is the I AM 1
1. I AM Who I AM: Exodus 3:14...3
2. I AM the God of Your Fathers: Exodus 3:15.....................................5
3. I AM the Righteous God: Leviticus 18:5..7
4. I AM the Holy God: Leviticus 20:26 9
5. Before Abraham Was, I AM: John 8:58..11

Section 2: I AM the Bread of Life...13
6. Bread of Life: John 6:35..15
7. Manna from Heaven: Exodus 16:4 17
8. Multiplied Loaves and Fishes: John 6:14 19
9. Eternal Bread: John 6:51 21
10. The Lord's Supper: John 6:56..23

Section 3: I AM the Light of the World 25
11. The Light of the World: John 8:12 27
12. Guided by God's Presence: Exodus 13:21......................................29
13. The Light Is in Him: John 1:4–5...31
14. Light or Darkness: John 3:19 33
15. Darkness in the World: Mark 15:33..35

Section 4: I AM the Door 37
16. The Door of the Sheep: John 10:7 39
17. The Door of Righteousness: Psalm 118:20 41
18. What Is the Door?: John 10:1–2..43
19. God Watches Over Us: Psalm 121:8 45
20. Jesus Stands at the Door: Revelation 3:20....................................47

Section 5: I AM the Good Shepherd 49
21. The Good Shepherd: John 10:14–15 51
22. The Seeking Shepherd: Ezekiel 34:11 53

23. The Sacrificial Shepherd: John 10:11 55
24. The Equipping Shepherd: Hebrews 13:20–21 57
25. The Sheep Know Him: John 10:27 59

Section 6: I AM the Way, the Truth, and the Life **61**
26. The Way, the Truth, and the Life: John 14:6 63
27. Grace and Truth: John 1:14 65
28. The Truth Will Set You Free: John 8:32 67
29. Abundant Life: John 10:10 69
30. The Purpose of Truth: John 18:37 71

Section 7: I AM the True Vine **73**
31. The True Vine: John 15:1 75
32. The Fruit of the Spirit: Galatians 5:22–23 77
33. Abide in Me: John 15:5 79
34. Glorify God: John 15:8–9 81
35. Bear Fruit: John 15:16 83

Section 8: I AM the Resurrection and the Life **85**
36. The Resurrection and the Life: John 11:25–26 87
37. He Has Borne Our Griefs: Isaiah 53:5 89
38. The Work of Redemption: 1 Corinthians 1:30 91
39. Resurrection and Newness: Romans 6:4–5 93
40. He Is Risen!: Matthew 28:6 95

About the Authors 97

Preface

Ways to Study *Jesus, the I AM*

How can you get the most out of this study for Lent? This study is designed to guide you through the forty days of Lent. It also has a four-week Bible-study curriculum that accompanies it for those who want to study this as a group.

As you study, consider using at least one of these suggestions to deepen your study:

1. Read the devotions provided for each week of Lent. Daily Bible study and personal reflection can give you the opportunity to mourn over Jesus's suffering and celebrate His resurrection.
2. Meditate on and/or memorize the verse included with each devotion.
3. Respond to the questions that accompany the devotions either in writing or mentally.
4. Enlist a study partner (or several) to join you on the journey.
5. Pray daily that God will use this journey to teach you more about how God and Jesus are the *I AM*.

Introduction

Jesus, the I AM

We all describe ourselves using words that reveal a part of who we are. For example, if I wanted you to recognize me at the airport before we've ever met in person, I might use words like older, female, dark hair, and blue eyes. Or I might instead describe what I would wear, such as a bright red coat and green hat, so I would be easier to identify.

If I tried to describe my personality, the words would be different. I might say that I'm task oriented, fun loving, and driven. Or I might choose to describe my hobbies, or my interests, or my family. Or I might share with you the things on my to-do list to show you where I spend my time.

All of these are ways to describe myself, but none of them complete the picture. Each word helps to paint a picture of who I am, but not a finished portrait.

Jesus chose to reveal His relationship to His Father, the Lord God Almighty. He used God's own words to Moses to connect His identity to His Father's. God identified Himself to Moses as "I AM WHO I AM" (Exodus 3:14). Jesus made seven statements that identify Him with the Father. Each begins with the acknowledgement—I AM. Jesus said:

- I AM the Bread of Life (John 6:35).
- I AM the Light of the World (John 8:12).
- I AM the Door (John 10:7).
- I AM the Good Shepherd (John 10:14).
- I AM the Way, the Truth, and the Life (John 14:6).
- I AM the True Vine (John 15:1).
- I AM the Resurrection and the Life (John 11:25).

During this season of Lent, through this study, delve into the identity of Jesus, the only Son of God who intentionally came to be with us, to love us, and to die for us, so that we could be restored in relationship with God. We pray this opportunity will guide you into a newer and deeper understanding of the divine identity of Jesus—the I AM.

Margie Williamson

Introduction
Jesus, the I AM

We all describe ourselves using words that reveal a part of who we are. For example, if I wanted you to recognize me at the airport before we've ever met in person, I might use words like older, female, dark hair, and blue eyes. Or I might instead describe what I would wear, such as a bright red coat and green hat, so I would be easier to identify.

If I tried to describe my personality, the words would be different. I might say that I'm task oriented, fun loving, and driven. Or I might choose to describe my hobbies, or my interests, or my family. Or I might share with you the things on my to-do list to show you where I spend my time.

All of these are ways to describe myself, but none of them complete the picture. Each word helps to paint a picture of who I am, but not a finished portrait.

Jesus chose to reveal His relationship to His Father, the Lord God Almighty. He used God's own words to Moses to connect His identity to His Father's. God identified Himself to Moses as "I AM WHO I AM" (Exodus 3:14). Jesus made seven statements that identify Him with the Father. Each begins with the acknowledgement—I AM. Jesus said:

- I AM the Bread of Life (John 6:35).
- I AM the Light of the World (John 8:12).
- I AM the Door (John 10:7).
- I AM the Good Shepherd (John 10:14).
- I AM the Way, the Truth, and the Life (John 14:6).
- I AM the True Vine (John 15:1).
- I AM the Resurrection and the Life (John 11:25).

During this season of Lent, through this study, delve into the identity of Jesus, the only Son of God who intentionally came to be with us, to love us, and to die for us, so that we could be restored in relationship with God. We pray this opportunity will guide you into a newer and deeper understanding of the divine identity of Jesus—the I AM.

Margie Williamson

SECTION 1

God Is the I AM

Margie Williamson

Day 1
I AM Who I AM

God said to Moses, "I AM WHO I AM." And he said, "Say this to the people of Israel: 'I AM has sent me to you.'"

—Exodus 3:14

I identify myself with a lot of statements that describe me. I am a Christian. I am a wife. I am a mother and a grandmother. I am a student. I am a writer. I am all of these things. Notice that all these statements are positive. I could just as easily list the things about myself that I'm still working on or the things that I am not. In actuality, *I am* statements are the sum total of who we are—our strengths and our weaknesses, our gifts and our challenges, our character and our personality.

Read Exodus 3:1–14. At the burning bush, Moses asked God what he was to tell the Israelites when they asked him what God's name was. There's been a lot of scholarly debate about what the proposed question really meant. Some suggest that the Israelites would want to know if *this God* was different from the pagan gods of the land. Other scholars suggest that the Israelites in Egypt knew the name *YHWH* (written Yahweh in English). Surely the people would have remembered the stories from the patriarchs about their God Yahweh. Therefore, asking for identification of the God who had been talked about for generations doesn't seem to fit the question.

Author and philosopher Martin Buber suggests that the question was about "the significance, character, quality, and interpretation of the name." He points out that what the Israelites' question really meant was, "What does the name *mean* and *signify* in circumstances such as we are in?"[1] Their circumstances had been terrible for years. They were held in slavery, put into forced labor, and their future was bleak. It makes sense, doesn't it, that they would want to know what difference this God was going to make in their lives then. They wanted to see God at work in their lives to bring about a change in those circumstances.

---

[1] Martin Buber, *Moses: The Revelation and the Covenant* (New York: Harper and Row, 1958), 48–55; quoted in *The Expositor's Bible Commentary*, v. 2, Frank E. Gaebelein (Grand Rapids: Zondervan Publishers, 1990), 320.

Respond

Can you relate to how the Israelites might have felt when Moses came to deliver God's message to them? Why?

_____

_____

_____

_____

Have you wondered where God is when your own circumstances seem hopeless?

_____

_____

_____

_____

Did you lose hope waiting for God's response? Why?

_____

_____

_____

_____

Read verse 14 again. Explain how God's name can bring hope to you when you feel hopeless.

_____

_____

_____

_____

Day 2
I AM the God of Your Fathers

God also said to Moses, "Say this to the people of Israel: 'The LORD, the God of your fathers, the God of Abraham, the God of Isaac, and the God of Jacob, has sent me to you.' This is my name forever, and thus I am to be remembered throughout all generations."

—Exodus 3:15

I have a heritage of faith that goes back through both sides of my family tree. Every year, one side of the family gets together for a reunion. We camp in the North Georgia mountains, and we plan a worship service for the Sunday we are together. That time of worship brings together those in the past who taught us, guided us, and brought us to faith. Our worship also focuses on what God is doing in our extended family. We've prayed over those whom God has called into ministry, and we've celebrated decisions children have made in baptism.

Read Exodus 3:15–20. God continued to tell Moses how to identify Him to the Israelites. In these verses, God responded with a history lesson. Note the word "also" in verse 15. God the I AM was also the God of the Israelites' past. He was the God who had been with their fathers Abraham, Isaac, and Jacob. He was the God who had been with them since the beginning. He was their God. And He would exist with them forever.

The phrase I AM can also be understood with the verb "to be." It shows the essence of who God is. And it points to God's promise: "I will be with you." Quite simply, God was and is the I AM. His purpose is to be with His people.

Think about what you know about God—His characteristics of mercy and forgiveness, His desire for a just and righteous world, His ability to love beyond measure. Think about who God is—He is the Creator and Designer of heaven and earth. He is the beginning and the end of everything. He is everything. He is *the* I AM.

Respond

Describe yourself with *I am* statements:

_____

_____

_____

_____

Describe how you see God with *You are* statements:

_____

_____

_____

_____

Compare these lists. Do you see how God has impacted your life through your own *I am* statements? Why? If not, why not?

_____

_____

_____

_____

Do your statements about who God is accurately reflect God the I AM? Why? Do these statements show how your understanding of God continues to grow? Why?

_____

_____

_____

_____

Day 3
I AM the Righteous God

"You shall therefore keep my statutes and my rules; if a person does them, he shall live by them: I am the LORD."

—Leviticus 18:5

Historically, in many parts of the country, churches were the centers of their communities. Family life was structured around their churches' times of worship, study, and prayer, and of opportunities to fellowship together. Churches impacted their communities to such a point that the south was known as the Bible Belt. Those days are long past. Churches today, not just in the south, now face cultural struggles from outside. As many churches' attendance declines, they are left trying to figure out how to impact the national and cultural conversations from a Christian worldview.

Read Leviticus 18:1–5. In Leviticus, God stressed what the culture of the people of Israel was to be. He reminded the people that they were not to take the culture and the beliefs of the Egyptians into the Promised Land. Even though they had lived in that culture for their entire lives, the people were expected to live by God's standards. God also informed the people that they were not to take on the culture and the beliefs of the people who already lived in the Promised Land. Sadly, much of the Old Testament deals with the Israelites' inability to stay apart from the pagan religious culture in Israel.

Why was God so determined that His people should live by His standards? Because God is a righteous God—He cannot abide unrighteousness. God hates evil and He hates disobedience. He hates seeing how people's lives and families can be destroyed through unrighteous living. It is because He is righteous that He wants His people to live righteous lives.

We become righteous through God's redemption. It's not something that we can achieve on our own. It comes from God and is a reflection of who He is. Because we have been made righteous in Christ, God expects us to live in a way that is different from those who are unbelievers. And by doing so, we allow others to see the very character of God lived out in our lives.

Respond

What does righteousness look like in the life of a believer?

_____
_____
_____
_____

How do you live righteously? Is righteous living a struggle for you? Why?

_____
_____
_____
_____

Read Psalm 1 and underline the descriptions of righteousness. Do these descriptors agree with what you've listed above? Why?

_____
_____
_____
_____

Based on what you've written above, does the way you live show others God's righteousness? Why?

_____
_____
_____
_____

Day 4
I AM the Holy God

"You shall be holy to me, for I the LORD am holy and have separated you from the peoples, that you should be mine."

—Leviticus 20:26

When my granddaughter made her profession of faith last year, she absolutely glowed with joy from her decision. She called me on a video call to tell me and she couldn't stop smiling. She was only six but she had been thinking about her decision for a long time. Imagine how she felt later that evening when her dad helped her understand that the decision she had made only had to be made once. She was shocked to know she didn't have to get up the next morning and do it all over again. That's the meaning of being redeemed and being made righteous in God. We make the decision to accept what He has already done for us through the death and resurrection of His Son, Jesus.

Read Leviticus 20:22–26. God also instructed the Israelites to be holy. Holiness is not given to us through redemption but is something we must choose to do. And it's something we should want to do because of what God has done for us. To be holy means to take on the character of God—being good and pure and godly and sacred. It's a decision a believer makes every day—to misquote Shakespeare, "To be holy or not to be holy, that is the question." Being holy is a process. It takes time, study, prayer, and discipline to be holy. Becoming holy is the result of growing closer to God in relationship with Him. It's making the choice to become more like Him and less like our humanity tells us to be.

Peter wrote: "As he who called you is holy, you also be holy in all your conduct, since it is written, 'You shall be holy, for I am holy'" (1 Pet. 1:15–16). For this holiness to take hold, God had one more instruction. In Leviticus 20:26, God explained that because the people belonged to Him, they would become holy like Him. We are to be holy as God Himself is holy.

Respond

How do you respond to God's holiness? Be specific.

_____

_____

_____

_____

Do you think others see God's holiness in you? Why?

_____

_____

_____

_____

How do you see God's holiness in yourself?

_____

_____

_____

_____

Could you explain to a new believer why becoming holy is an important part of being a Christian? Why?

_____

_____

_____

_____

Day 5
Before Abraham Was, I AM

Jesus said to them, "Truly, truly, I say to you, before Abraham was, I am."

—John 8:58

Before I made my appearance in this world, generations of relatives preceded me. Some were outstanding men and women of faith. Some were not. Regardless, I carry their DNA within me—even those ancestors whom I know nothing about. They all came before me. They came ahead of me. They preceded me.

Read John 8:48–58. The Pharisees were ready to argue with Jesus. At question was Jesus's true identity. The Pharisees couldn't believe the things that Jesus had said about Himself. They threw accusations at Jesus. They claimed Jesus was a Samaritan, a half-bred Jew. Or He was a demon using evil powers. Maybe He was a liar and everything He had claimed was false. Or, worse, He was an imposter, pretending to be someone He wasn't.

Jesus brought their questions and their arguments to the real point behind them. Jesus questioned who their father was. The Pharisees and the religious leaders and even the Jews themselves looked to Father Abraham as the beginning of their faith. Abraham was held in the highest esteem. Jesus responded that even before Abraham came into the world, Jesus had existed. Jesus came before Abraham. Jesus preceded Abraham because He came according to the plan of His Father—the one and only Almighty God.

Abraham lived and died. He was human. Jesus lived, died, and was resurrected. He was and is the Son of God who has existed for all time. Abraham was promised that generations of people would come from his lineage. Jesus came as the promise for all people.

Respond

The Pharisees were confused about Jesus's identity, and they looked for evidence that fit their preconceived understanding of Him. What evidence do you see of that happening in the world today? Why do you think some people struggle with correctly understanding who Jesus is?

_____

_____

_____

Have you ever had to defend Jesus as the Son of God? Remember what that experience was like? Would you do it differently if you had to do it all over again? Why?

_____

_____

_____

Have you ever considered the question behind Jesus's response to the Pharisees: Who is your spiritual Father? Do you depend upon that Father? Why?

_____

_____

_____

Read verse 58 again. Reflect on how knowing that Jesus existed before all mankind impacts your understanding of God.

_____

_____

_____

SECTION 2

I AM the Bread of Life

Margie Williamson

Day 6
Bread of Life

Jesus said to them, "I am the bread of life; whoever comes to me shall not hunger, and whoever believes in me shall never thirst."

—John 6:35

Early in our marriage (mainly before children), life was simple and we had more time to try out new hobbies. I remember one year we took a two-week vacation to my parents' cabin in the North Georgia mountains. We spent our time relaxing and catching up on reading. And I learned to bake bread—the real way, by adding yeast and kneading the dough several times, letting it rise in a warm spot. This was long before bread machines that did all the manual labor for you. When the bread came out of the oven, it smelled amazing and tasted even better.

Making bread was a daily chore for the women in the first century. Every day, they made bread from scratch, using a bit of the leavened dough from the day before as a starter. It wasn't a luxury item but was rather a necessary part of their survival. The bread they made kept their families nourished for a day. Their bread gave them physical life.

Read John 6:30–40. Just before this encounter between Jesus and the crowd who had followed Him across the Sea of Galilee, Jesus had fed five thousand men plus women and children. It was miraculous. Yet, the next day, the same people who had been fed from Jesus's miraculous power asked when He was going to do something that would prove He was God's Son. You'd think feeding thousands of people from almost nothing would have been enough. But it wasn't.

Moses had fed the people daily with God's bread from heaven. Jesus responded to what could have been an infuriating question and explained that the bread of heaven had been a gift from God, not Moses. And that bread had only fed their physical bodies. Now, Jesus said, God had given them spiritual bread that would give them eternal life. And that bread was His own body.

Respond

Can you imagine being on site when Jesus fed thousands of people with only two loaves of bread and five small fishes? Do you think you could have witnessed that in person and still want to see Jesus do something miraculous? Why?

_____

_____

_____

_____

_____

As the Bread of Life, Jesus was again showing His divinity and His relationship with His Father. How does the Bread of Life meet the deepest needs of mankind?

_____

_____

_____

_____

_____

Read verse 38 again. Why was Jesus stating that He is the true Bread of Life?

_____

_____

_____

_____

_____

Day 7
Manna from Heaven

> Then the LORD said to Moses, "Behold, I am about to rain bread from heaven for you, and the people shall go out and gather a day's portion every day, that I may test them, whether they will walk in my law or not."
>
> —Exodus 16:4

In seminary, my husband, Bob, and I lived in a furnished, one-bedroom apartment on campus. We owned only a rocking chair and the boards and concrete blocks to hold the stereo system. When Bob graduated, he was called to a church in Savannah, Georgia. Church members found us a fully furnished, historic townhouse to live in for our first three months in the city. Obviously, it didn't take us long to unpack. But when we walked into the kitchen, we found the church had held a "pounding" for us—something that was a custom in many Baptist churches once upon a time. On top of the counters and inside the cupboards were pounds and pounds of dry goods and canned goods. I have never seen such abundance anywhere outside of a grocery store. Poor as we were coming straight out of seminary, those gifts of foods blessed us daily for months and months and enabled us to purchase a home and begin to furnish it.

Read Exodus 16:3–21. When the Hebrews left Egypt, they had to leave behind much of what they owned. They left their houses and the furniture, their livelihoods, and their sense of safety. Even though they had lived in slavery, they understood that world. They knew the rules. They knew where their next meal would come from. As they left Egypt, they focused on the things they no longer had. And the farther they went, the more they grumbled about the things they left behind. Much of their frustration focused on not knowing where their next meal would come from.

God rained bread down on the Hebrews. The bread was more than just food to eat. The manna from heaven daily demonstrated that God was in control and that He was taking care of them along the journey. That bread symbolized the relationship between God and His people. And it was a daily reminder that He alone could meet all their needs.

Respond

Have you ever been treated with gifts in such abundance that you were speechless? How did that outpouring of gifts make you feel?

_____

_____

_____

_____

_____

Look up "Manna from Heaven" on your digital device. How is it described?

_____

_____

_____

_____

Unfortunately, the Hebrews were not always grateful for God's provision of manna. They continued to gripe and ask for more. Have you ever become dissatisfied by God's provision in your life? What caused the dissatisfaction? How did you move beyond it?

_____

_____

_____

_____

_____

Day 8
Multiplied Loaves and Fishes

When the people saw the sign that he had done, they said, "This is indeed the Prophet who is to come into the world!"

—John 6:14

The first scripture passage I memorized was the Lord's Prayer from Matthew 6. I think I learned it the year I was baptized, and it became the foundation of what I understand about God. I didn't really understand a lot of it. At seven years old, I wasn't concerned about the kingdom that was to come and temptation wasn't much of a struggle. But what I learned was that God has providence over our lives. He cares for us. He knows our needs and takes care of them through His provision.

Read John 6:1–14. Jesus had been teaching His disciples near the shore of Galilee when He looked up and saw thousands of people headed toward Him. John recorded that five thousand people were there. Actually, the scripture only refers to the men who came, so thousands more—both women and children—were also there. The crowd must have gathered spontaneously because no one had brought provisions with them. No one, that is, except a small boy whose mom had packed his lunch. The child had five small loaves of bread and two small fishes, possibly sardines or something similarly tiny. His mother had made the bread and salted the fish to keep it from rotting. She had done her best to take care of her son.

The approaching multitudes, however, had nothing. Jesus recognized their needs and asked Philip where they could buy food for them all. For Jesus, this was one of those teachable moments for His disciples. He knew they couldn't afford to purchase that much food. But, by testing Philip with the question, Jesus had the opportunity to meet the need He saw in a way that honored God. It's hard to know how the disciples expected Jesus to meet this need, but it certainly wasn't that Jesus would divinely turn a small boy's lunch into food that would feed thousands.

Respond

Have you been in a position where you were really hungry and had no way to get food where you were? What did you end up doing?

_____

_____

_____

Imagine being one of the disciples who watched the small loaves of bread and two fishes feed thousands of people. Read the passage again. What physical actions did Jesus take? What did Jesus not do?

_____

_____

_____

What lesson do you think Jesus was ultimately teaching His disciples?

_____

_____

_____

Do you think Jesus's feeding of the thousands reminded the Jews of how God had provided for them during the Exodus from Egypt? Why?

_____

_____

_____

Day 9
Eternal Bread

"I am the living bread that came down from heaven. If anyone eats of this bread, he will live forever. And the bread that I will give for the life of the world is my flesh."

—John 6:51

Over the years, I've been fascinated by the stories of people who claimed to be Jesus. There were many who made that claim. The roll includes names like Jim Jones, David Koresh, Charles Manson, and Marshall Applewhite. Jim Jones led his followers in the largest mass suicide in American history. David Koresh claimed to be the son of God and required all women and girls to be his wives. Charles Manson is known for his evilness in leading his followers to commit at least five murders. Marshall Applewhite created the Heaven's Gate cult that required its members to commit suicide in order to be taken up on an alien spacecraft. None of these men lived godly lives. None represented the teachings of God. All of them took the lives of their followers. Yet time after time, people were drawn to them and accepted their claims.

Read John 6:41–51. Unlike the false claimants above, Jesus always presented Himself as who He was. But the religious leaders couldn't accept His identity and complained about what He said. In the conversation in these verses, Jesus compared His life and sacrifice to the gift from God that the Jews accepted—God's manna from heaven. The word *manna* can be translated as "What is it?" Manna was something mysterious that came from heaven in the night and waited for them each morning. Jesus came from heaven to live among the people and to give His life for them. Like picking up manna each morning, all the people had to do was accept Jesus's gift of salvation.

In every point, Jesus is greater than the gift of manna. God's manna from heaven was designed to give physical life for a day. Jesus's sacrificial gift gives spiritual life for eternity. God's manna cost God nothing personally, but Jesus's sacrifice was extremely costly—even to the point of death.

Respond

Reflect on the phrase, "I am the living bread that came down from heaven." How does that describe the intentionality of God sending His Son to earth for us?

_____

_____

_____

Reread verse 44. How have you seen God intentionally draw you to Him?

_____

_____

_____

Jesus pointed out that He alone had seen God the Father (v. 46). How does that give evidence of the relationship of God the Father, Jesus the Son, and the Holy Spirit?

_____

_____

_____

If you've accepted the eternal bread of Christ, how would you describe that gift to someone who hasn't? If you haven't accepted Christ, why not?

_____

_____

_____

Day 10
The Lord's Supper

"Whoever feeds on my flesh and drinks my blood abides in me, and I in him."

—John 6:56

When I was a teenager, I was a bit interested in boys. (Yeah, that's probably an understatement.) One Sunday evening I was in church waiting for the Lord's Supper service to begin. I was also sitting between two young men, one I'd had a date with that afternoon and the other I was going out with after the service. I was having a really good time, enjoying the attention I was receiving. But a college student sitting behind me tapped me on the shoulder and handed me his Bible that was opened to the Luke 14 passage about the Lord's Supper. "Read this," he said to me. "I think you've forgotten why we're here tonight." I was mortified and embarrassed. And I knew he was right. What we do during the Lord's Supper has great significance to us as believers and should not ever be taken lightly.

Read John 6:52–56. The Jews listening to Jesus's words here had no idea what He was talking about. They thought Jesus meant that they would have to literally eat His flesh and drink His blood. It's no wonder they were confused. These Jews had no spiritual ability to interpret Jesus's statement. In fact, Jewish law strictly forbade eating human flesh or drinking blood of any kind. Notice, though, that Jesus repeated the command to eat His flesh and drink His blood three times. The fact that Jesus made that statement three times demonstrates how important it was. But Jesus wasn't speaking literally about flesh and blood.

Jesus didn't institute the Lord's Supper until the last night He was with His disciples. Yet, at this earlier point in His ministry, Jesus presented the foundational truth of the Lord's Supper to the Jews who questioned what He said. Warren Wiersbe sums it up this way: "All Jesus said [to the Jews] was, 'Just as you take food and drink within your body and it becomes a part of you, so you must receive Me within your innermost being so that I can give you life.'"[2] With spiritual eyes, believers can understand that we symbolically eat of His body and drink of His blood through the Lord's Supper as a reminder of what He has done for us.

---

[2] Warren Wiersbe, *The Bible Exposition Commentary: New Testament*, v. 1 (Colorado Springs, CO: David C. Cook, 1989), 312.

Respond

Do you think the Jews were unable to hear what Jesus was saying because they filtered everything through the laws they had lived by for generations? Why?

_____

_____

_____

_____

_____

_____

Have traditions and beliefs you've been taught over the years made it difficult for you to hear spiritual truth? Why?

_____

_____

_____

_____

_____

_____

How does participating in the Lord's Supper impact you spiritually? How does it impact you in worship? How does it impact you emotionally? Why?

_____

_____

_____

_____

_____

_____

SECTION 3

I AM the Light of the World

Margie Williamson

Day 11
The Light of the World

Again Jesus spoke to them, saying, "I am the light of the world. Whoever follows me will not walk in darkness, but will have the light of life."

—John 8:12

Moving to that historic house in Savannah was an experience for us. The humidity there attracts thousands of palmetto bugs, a large ugly roach-like bug. The palmetto bugs are specifically attracted to areas such as bathrooms and kitchens. We didn't know the bugs existed at all, much less lived in our leased townhome, until we went back into the kitchen after we'd already gone upstairs for the night. When we flipped on the overhead kitchen light, it looked like the floor and cabinets were moving as what seemed like hundreds of those large roaches ran to their hiding places behind the fridge and under the sink. In the three months we lived there, I don't think we ever again went back downstairs at night. There was nothing we could do to control the bugs, so we avoided them at all costs.

John began his gospel account with a statement that describes Jesus: "In him was life, and the life was the light of men. The light shines in the darkness, and the darkness has not overcome it" (John 1:4–5). Read John 8:12–20. The verses just before these tell of the woman who was caught in adultery and brought before Jesus. The religious leaders wanted Jesus to pass a death verdict on the woman. Instead, Jesus sent her away in grace. Then, in these verses, Jesus proclaimed that He is the light of the world. Using the metaphor of light, Jesus stated that He not only is the light Himself, but He brought light to the entire world.

The evil in this world runs when divine light is aimed at it. Jesus is that light which shines in that dark world. His is the only light that can reach that world's dark places and hidden crevices. His is the only light that can block out the world's darkness completely. And His is the only light that can offer grace, forgiveness, and restoration to bring the world back to God.

Respond

How would you describe the darkness of the world? Do you think that the darkness is worse today than it was in years past? Why?

_____

_____

_____

_____

Reflect on Jesus's teachings recorded throughout the Gospels. How did He offer forgiveness to the sinful?

_____

_____

_____

_____

When did Jesus confront evil directly? Does Jesus have ultimate power over evil? Why?

_____

_____

_____

_____

In your opinion, does your life reflect Jesus's light? Why do you think that?

_____

_____

_____

_____

Day 12
Guided by God's Presence

And the LORD went before them by day in a pillar of cloud to lead them along the way, and by night in a pillar of fire to give them light, that they might travel by day and by night.

—Exodus 13:21

My younger grandchildren, Ava and Caleb, just watched fireworks in person for the first time. They were completely mesmerized by the bright colors that filled the skies and loved the different patterns of the explosions. They "oohed" and "aahed" over each explosion as the finale came along. Ava, the oldest, needed to know where the fireworks came from and how they worked. Caleb, three years younger, just accepted them as "big, colorful, and glittery." Both agreed that the sight of the fireworks in the night sky was amazing. What they saw, however, cannot compare to the light the Hebrews followed from Egypt.

Read Exodus 13:17–22. As the Hebrews were led away from Egypt on their journey to the Promised Land, they were led by God's presence. During the day, they were led by God's presence in a pillar of cloud that guided them and covered them in shade to protect them from the hot desert sun. During the night, they were led by God's presence in a pillar of fire which cast light on them. Between the pillar of cloud and the pillar of fire, the people were able to travel safely during the day or at night. And God's presence never left them, guiding them all the way. In fact, Exodus 40:34–38 shares that when the pillars didn't move, neither did the people.

What's interesting about the pillar of fire is that, while the Hebrews could see where they were going by its light, the Egyptians could not. Warren Wiersbe explains that the pillar moved between the Hebrews and the Egyptians, giving light and protection to the Hebrews, "but darkness to the enemy."[3] God's light for the Hebrews gave them the ability to see where they were going. It also hid the enemy from their eyes. And it faithfully guided them for the forty years they spent wandering in the wilderness.

---

3 Warren Wiersbe, *The Bible Exposition Commentary: Old Testament*, v. 1 (Colorado Springs, CO: David C. Cook, 1989), 205.

Respond

Do you feel safer in lighted areas? Why?

_____

_____

_____

_____

What makes you feel unsafe in areas that are dark or poorly lit? Are your feelings justified? Why?

_____

_____

_____

_____

Do you think God's presence in the pillar of fire was a foreshadowing of Jesus bringing light to the world? Why or why not?

_____

_____

_____

_____

Has being a follower of Christ allowed you to live your life in light rather than darkness? Why is that?

_____

_____

_____

_____

Day 13
The Light Is in Him

> In him was life, and the life was the light of men. The light shines
> in the darkness, and the darkness has not overcome it.
>
> —John 1:4–5

I loved having fairy tales read to me when I was a child. They all seemed to begin the same way: "Once upon a time . . ." Those were magical words to me. I knew the story would unfold, creating a visual picture that I could see in my mind. I also knew that no matter what happened in the middle of the story—such as problems coming up or villains entering the story—it would always end with everything working out. Right would always prevail and the characters would live "happily ever after." It was years before I truly understood how unrealistically life was presented in these tales. In fact, by the very definition of fairy tales, the stories are overly idealized, the characters are overly perfect, and the endings are overly sweet.

Read John 1:1–5. John began to tell Jesus's story by using the words, "In the beginning . . ." Jesus's story was no fairy tale. His story doesn't tell of what could not possibly be real, but rather of what is real. In the beginning, God created the world, and Jesus was at His side. From the beginning, God had a plan that Jesus would come to earth to live with us. And, in Jesus was the light that would bring the world out of darkness. Isaiah, in his prophecy of Jesus's coming to earth, wrote,

> The people who walked in darkness
>   have seen a great light;
> those who dwelt in a land of deep darkness,
>   on them has light shone." (Isaiah 9:2)

John's writing was divinely inspired, especially in these first verses. John understood the basis of Jesus's light in the world in a way that could only have been given to him by God. John recognized that Jesus came to be the light that shined brightly into the dark world, the light that could defeat the darkness, and the light that would bring all men before God. Jesus's story is no fairy tale but is one of divine power and purpose.

Respond

When you hear a story begin with the statement, "Once upon a time," what do you expect from it?

_____

_____

_____

_____

How did you come to the realization that the world was not a simple place to live in? Did it happen in childhood or later?

_____

_____

_____

_____

Are you aware of the darkness of the world today? How can you explain this darkness?

_____

_____

_____

_____

How will Jesus ultimately defeat the power of evil in the world?

_____

_____

_____

_____

Day 14
Light or Darkness

And this is the judgment: the light has come into the world, and people loved the darkness rather than the light because their works were evil.

—John 3:19

As I get older, my skin more and more shows my age. But my eyesight is not as good, so I have trouble seeing the small marks, the little lines, and tiny blemishes. My two best tools have become a magnifying mirror and a really bright light. If I look in a mirror that doesn't magnify, I don't see those imperfections. But, when I use the magnifying mirror and a bright light, my flaws are clearly apparent. I can't help but think that our spiritual lives can be much the same. If we don't take time to look at ourselves closely, to examine ourselves in a bright light for our flaws, it can be easy not to acknowledge those spiritual flaws.

Chapter 3 of John begins with the story of Nicodemus, a Pharisee and a leader of the Jews, coming at night to talk to Jesus. Nicodemus probably came during the night so other Jews would not see him seek out Jesus. He used the darkness to hide what he was doing. Read John 3:16–21. Many biblical scholars believe that these verses were part of the conversation between Nicodemus and Jesus. If so, it's easier to understand Jesus's use of the ideas of "light" and "darkness." Jesus explained that people are comfortable in the dark—they can keep their sins hidden and no one has to know about them.

Those hidden sins are exactly what Jesus came to save us from. Jesus knows those sins. Regardless of what others know about us, Jesus knows the truth. And as Jesus explained to Nicodemus, Jesus came to earth because He loves us, despite the sins we try so desperately to keep hidden. Believers are not different from nonbelievers because believers have no sin. Rather, believers are different because they've brought their sins into the light of Jesus's redeeming love. Believers have accepted Jesus's redemption from sin, His restoration into God's presence, and His promise of eternity.

Respond

Have you noticed a difference in the way people act when others are looking and when they think no one can see them? Why do you think that is?

_____

_____

_____

_____

_____

Do you have things in your life that you keep hidden from people? Why?

_____

_____

_____

_____

_____

Did you know that many believers have at least one sin in their past that they think Jesus's redemption can't cover or forgive? Do you share that perspective? Where does your inability to accept Jesus's complete forgiveness come from?

_____

_____

_____

_____

_____

Day 15
Darkness in the World

And when the sixth hour had come, there was darkness over the whole land until the ninth hour.

—Mark 15:33

I used to teach teenagers in Bible study. One year at Easter, we were studying Mark 15 and I wanted to help the students experience the resurrection from a new perspective. I used black trash bags to block out the light coming in through the windows. I placed three unlit candles in the middle of the room. Then, I welcomed the students in and we talked about what it feels to be in the dark. After discussion, I lit the three candles and asked, "If Jesus had not been resurrected from the dead, would the world have remained in darkness?" Afterward, we removed the black coverings from the windows and let the morning light pour into the room. It turned out to be a remarkable experience, not just for the students but for me as well.

Read Mark 15:33–39. This passage powerfully looks at the concepts of "darkness" and "light" from a different perspective. John included one thing in his gospel that the other gospel writers didn't include. Mark recorded that at 12 noon, when the sun should have been at its most intense, the world became dark. That darkness wasn't like what is experienced when we have an eclipse. Rather, it lasted for three straight hours. And, during that time the world was dark.

The darkness over the earth was physical. But without Jesus's resurrection, that darkness would have been spiritual. Without Jesus's resurrection, Jesus's death would have been meaningless. Without Jesus's resurrection, the world would never have had a way into God's presence. Without Jesus's resurrection, Jesus's light would have been darkened. Jesus is the light that pushes away the darkness. He is the light that illuminates God's holiness. And Jesus is the one and only light that can redeem us and bring us into eternal life with Him.

Respond

How does sitting in the dark make you feel?

_____

_____

_____

_____

_____

_____

Describe how Easter Sunday commemorates the light of Jesus's resurrection.

_____

_____

_____

_____

_____

_____

If Jesus had not been resurrected from the dead, what would that do to your own conversion experience?

_____

_____

_____

_____

_____

_____

SECTION 4

I AM the Door

Benjie Shaw

Day 16
The Door of the Sheep

So Jesus again said to them, "Truly, truly, I say to you, I am the door of the sheep."

—John 10:7

Whenever I approach a new place, the door is one of the first things for which I look. I might notice a nice awning, a creative sign, or porch décor. But, ultimately, I'm looking for the door so that I can enter. I'm looking for the door because my only intentions are to be a customer of a business or to visit with the people who live in the home. Because I have no ulterior motive, I don't even consider other entrances. The front door serves my purposes perfectly.

Read John 10:7–10. Jesus made a similar observation at the beginning of John 10. He observed that only thieves and robbers attempt to enter a sheepfold by any means other than the door. Only the shepherd enters through the door. The gatekeeper will only let the shepherd in. The sheep will only respond to the voice of the shepherd. In fact, sheep will flee the voice of a stranger. But they will follow the voice of the shepherd in and out of the door of the sheepfold. Jesus is the door to the sheepfold. The sheepfold was a place of security, rest, and intimacy. Sheep could only enter the sheepfold by the door.

In the same way, Christians enter into a place of security, rest, and intimacy with the Father through Jesus. There is no other door by which we can enter this place of fellowship with God. Any who claim to have gotten there by other means make a false claim. By laying down His life for the sheep, Jesus is the only legitimate door through which we can enter to have true security, rest, and intimacy with God.

Respond

Have you tried other "doors" in hopes of finding God? What were the outcomes?

_____

_____

_____

_____

What about Jesus qualifies Him to be the only legitimate "door" to the Father?

_____

_____

_____

_____

How have you experienced the security, rest, and intimacy of the sheepfold?

_____

_____

_____

_____

How have you heard your shepherd calling you in the past? What does His voice sound like?

_____

_____

_____

_____

Day 17
The Door of Righteousness

This is the gate of the LORD;
    the righteous shall enter through it.

—Psalm 118:20

Blind spots were a difficult concept for me to understand when I was learning to drive. I understood the idea conceptually, but when push came to shove, I struggled to remember that the side-view mirror might not show me everything that was going on around me. It took a few close calls before the concept connected to my habits: just because I couldn't see a car there didn't mean that there wasn't a car there.

Read Psalm 118:19–20. The psalmist pleaded with the Lord to "open the gates of righteousness" so that he could enter in. He recognized that only God could open the gates to His own city. No person could earn his or her own way into God's city through their own righteousness. Interestingly, the psalmist observed that once the gate is opened "the righteous shall enter through it." In the course of God opening the gates of His city, something had happened to the person who would enter. By recognizing that only God possessed the righteousness needed to enter His city, the psalmist suggested the key to its entrance was found.

We all tend to have blind spots when evaluating ourselves. We tend to think more highly of ourselves than we ought. While identifying the ill intent or faults of others comes easily to us, we tend to rationalize our own behavior or poor treatment of others. In the back of our minds, we inflate our own righteousness over that of others. But the standard against which we are measured is not how our righteousness compares with other people's. The standard is God's righteousness. This is a standard that no one can ever measure up to outside of Jesus. We need God to open the door of righteousness for us to have any hope of entering into His city, His presence. Thanks be to God that He has made a way for us to enter in through Christ!

Respond

When was the last time you had a near miss with a blind spot?

_____

_____

_____

_____

What could motivate God to open the gates of righteousness to unrighteous people?

_____

_____

_____

_____

Why do you think we tend to rationalize our unrighteousness while being critical of the failings of others?

_____

_____

_____

_____

When was the last time you expressed praise to God for opening the door of righteousness through Jesus? Take a few minutes to do it now.

_____

_____

_____

_____

Day 18
What Is the Door?

Truly, truly, I say to you, he who does not enter the sheepfold by the door but climbs in by another way, that man is a thief and a robber. But he who enters by the door is the shepherd of the sheep.

—John 10:1–2

Social media regularly comes up with wacky challenges for people to participate in. This morning I came across the "Jeep Challenge." In the challenge, Jeep owners roll down the window of the driver's side door of their vehicle while keeping the door closed. Instead of opening the door and sitting down, Jeep owners attempt to enter the vehicle by doing a handstand against the driver's side door, sliding their feet into the door, and then performing a sit-up using the open window for leverage until they are able to slide into the driver's seat.

Read John 10:1–2. Jesus told His listeners that the person who enters the sheepfold by any means other than the door is "a thief and a robber." One who has to climb in over a wall, knock down a section of the wall, or find some other creative means of getting into the sheepfold probably isn't supposed to be there in the first place and is probably ill intentioned. Conversely, the shepherd of the sheep enters by the door. The shepherd has no ulterior motive or ill purpose to hide. He is there to tend the sheep and his entrance is likely welcome.

We often wonder if the voice to which we are listening belongs to Jesus or to something or someone else. In his classic work *Experiencing God*, Henry Blackaby identified four primary ways that God enters into our lives to speak to us: the Bible, prayer, circumstances, and the church.[4] Is the voice that you're listening to outside of any of those means of God speaking? If so, it's unlikely that it is the voice of Jesus. Lean into His Word. Seek Him in prayer. Rely on the wisdom of others in the church to help you discern what He's saying through your circumstances. He enters our lives to speak to us through these means.

---

[4] Henry Blackaby, *Experiencing God: Knowing and Doing the Will of God* (Nashville: B&H Publishers, 2008), 57.

Respond

What is the most "creative" way you've ever had to get into a car or building?

_____

_____

_____

_____

Which of the four ways in which God speaks do you most regularly hear from Him?

_____

_____

_____

_____

Do you struggle to hear from God in any of the four ways that He speaks? Why do you think you struggle with that one?

_____

_____

_____

_____

How does knowing how God speaks help us rule out competing voices?

_____

_____

_____

_____

Day 19
God Watches Over Us

The LORD will keep
    your going out and your coming in
    from this time forth and forevermore.

—Psalm 121:8

One of the blessings of COVID life has been the opportunities it has afforded my wife and me to reconnect with old friends. Zoom dates with college friends and catch-up conversations with friends from seminary have become a more regular occurrence during this season of life. Usually, these conversations involve retelling stories from our time together with our friends. Sharing these stories seems to serve as a way to remember the bond we have with each other and, in some strange way, solidifies an even deeper bond going forward. Taking the time to remember where we've been with friends plays an important role in our ongoing relationship with them.

Read Psalm 121:8. This psalm was sung by the Israelites as they ascended the mountain on their way into Jerusalem, likely for one of their major religious festivals. Throughout the psalm, the psalmist led Israel to remember the ways in which God had acted on their behalf in the past. Even though Israel's history was steeped in tragedy and difficult circumstances, the act of remembering how God had acted to preserve and help them, both as a nation and as individuals, was meant to encourage their faith and prepare them to worship God in Jerusalem.

Sometimes our struggles can make us wonder if God hears us. We may wonder if He's really there or if He's asleep while we struggle. In those moments, our task is to remember how God has come through for us in the past, both in saving us and in caring for us in our daily needs. Jesus is the Good Shepherd who watches over our going out and our coming in with care and compassion. Our help comes from Him. Our task is simply to come to Him as our shepherd and allow Him to care for us.

Respond

Are shared stories of the past an important part in your relationships with old friends? Why?

_____

_____

_____

_____

Describe a time when you have experienced God watching over you recently.

_____

_____

_____

_____

What circumstances make you doubt whether or not God is watching over you?

_____

_____

_____

_____

How can you intentionally remind yourself of God's care for you when you're struggling?

_____

_____

_____

_____

Day 20
Jesus Stands at the Door

Behold, I stand at the door and knock. If anyone hears my voice and opens the door, I will come in to him and eat with him, and he with me.

—Revelation 3:20

Going to someone's house for the first time can sometimes make me feel anxious. Not one to normally obsess over details, I will check the address three or four times before entering it into my phone. Upon arriving, I look for any other verification possible that I'm at the correct house. I make sure I recognize the car. I look for a sign that has the family's name either on the mailbox, the door, or somewhere else on the exterior. If any of these are present, I feel better about actually knocking on the door. All of those anxious feelings are swept away when the door is opened and I'm welcomed into the home.

Read Revelation 3:16–20. While we often use this verse in the context of evangelism, Jesus originally spoke it to a church. These were people who had already professed faith in Jesus, but their faith was "lukewarm" (v. 16). They were instructed to "be zealous and repent" (v. 19). The church's faith had already grown dim. Members needed to repent. Jesus reminded them that He was the one knocking at the door. All they had to do was open that door and allow Him in.

Repentance isn't a once-for-all action that we take when we profess faith in Jesus. Repentance is a posture of the heart that daily acknowledges our dependence on the grace of God in Christ. All of us, no matter how long we have followed Jesus, still sin daily. A heart that walks in a posture of repentance makes a practice of confessing sin. Jesus stands at the door and knocks. His invitation to eat with Him is extended to those who walk in a posture of repentance and dependence. Have you welcomed Him in?

Respond

What kinds of verification do you look for when you go to someone's house for the first time?

_____

_____

_____

_____

How have you heard Revelation 3:20 referred to in the past? Has the connection to repentance ever been made?

_____

_____

_____

_____

Why do we need to regularly repent of sin?

_____

_____

_____

_____

What habits or practices can help you make a practice of confessing and repenting of sin?

_____

_____

_____

_____

SECTION 5

I AM the Good Shepherd

Benjie Shaw

Day 21
The Good Shepherd

I am the good shepherd. I know my own and my own know me, just as the Father knows me and I know the Father; and I lay down my life for the sheep.

—John 10:14–15

A large church near where I live opened up a massive indoor playground. A whole section of the church is filled with tunnels, rope obstacles, places for kids to climb cargo nets, and tons of slides. I took my daughter for the first time a few years ago. Apart from how much she loved it, I was struck by how difficult it was for me to keep track of her in the crowd of other children and the sea of play obstacles even when I was vigilant. When she was quiet and concentrating, keeping track of her was almost impossible. But one thing always helped me hone in on where she was: her voice. Anytime I heard her voice I could instantly locate exactly where she was on the course and among the crowd.

Read John 10:14–15. Jesus shows He is the Good Shepherd by His knowledge of us. We show that we are His sheep by our knowledge of Him. But Jesus's standing as the Good Shepherd goes beyond just His knowledge of us. Jesus is the Good Shepherd because He gave His life to save His sheep.

A shepherd was tasked with caring for sheep at any cost. Good shepherds took great risk to protect or even rescue sheep that had wandered away or fallen into the clutches of predators. In 1 Samuel 17:34–36, King David recalled how as a shepherd boy, he had confronted both lions and bears to save sheep entrusted to his care. Jesus took His care for His sheep even further by willingly giving up His life to save them from their sin. Jesus doesn't just know you. Jesus knows you, loves you, and demonstrates this love by willingly laying down His life to redeem you from your sin.

Jesus, the I AM

Respond

Is there one person's voice in your life that you can always pick out in a crowd? Whose is it? What is it about that voice that allows you to do this?

_____

_____

_____

_____

Why is it important that Jesus both knows and loves us?

_____

_____

_____

_____

How has Jesus demonstrated that He is the Good Shepherd in your life?

_____

_____

_____

_____

How do you hear Jesus's voice?

_____

_____

_____

_____

Day 22
The Seeking Shepherd

For thus says the Lord GOD: Behold, I, I myself will search for my sheep and will seek them out.

—Ezekiel 34:11

My son's favorite toy when he was learning to walk and talk was a red race car whose driver was Mickey Mouse. In his little, infant voice, he affectionately called it "Mickey Mouse Race Car." He loved playing with it so much that it was regularly the first thing he asked for when he woke up in the morning and from his afternoon nap. Anytime it would go missing, which happened pretty often, my wife and I would search the house and our cars high and low to find Mickey Mouse Race Car because it was our son's most prized possession, the thing on which he had set his heart and affection.

Read Ezekiel 34:11–16. God's people had been led by religious shepherds who were not properly caring for them. Instead of feeding the sheep, these shepherds gorged themselves. Instead of protecting the sheep, they protected themselves. In response, God promised that He would personally come to seek His sheep. He would personally care for them by leading them out of danger and into a safe pasture to graze. God would personally tend to the sheep who were injured, sick, or weak while promising judgment on those who made themselves comfortable at His sheep's expense.

We sometimes feel isolated from God when we see others doing well. We wonder if God cares for us or if He even sees us. But we can be confident that not only does God see us and value us, He promises to come after us to care for us when we are struggling, harassed, and helpless. He has set His affection on us as His people and will stop at nothing until we are cared for, our wounds are bound up, and we are grazing in His pasture in peace. When we stray, God will always seek us out because we are His joy and prize.

Respond

What was the one toy you always had to have when you were a kid? Did you ever lose it? What happened?

_____

_____

_____

_____

What motivates a shepherd to stop caring for his/her sheep and seek personal comfort?

_____

_____

_____

_____

How does God personally seek after His sheep when they wander or stray?

_____

_____

_____

_____

Why does God care so much about individual sheep?

_____

_____

_____

_____

Day 23
The Sacrificial Shepherd

"I am the good shepherd. The good shepherd lays down his life for the sheep."

—John 10:11

I was a senior in high school on 9/11. Uncertainty reigned in the days and weeks afterwards. One of the primary questions that concerned my dad, himself a veteran, was whether or not a draft would be instituted. Dad had always told me that when I turned 18, I would either go to college, get a job, or join the Army, with the understanding that the final two options weren't real options for me. But, in the wake of 9/11, Dad determined that if a draft was instituted, he would reenlist, thus saving me from a draft. He was willing to sacrifice his own plans and desires to give me the opportunity to go to college and build a different kind of life for myself.

Read John 10:11–13. Jesus saved us from the danger and consequences of sin by laying down His life on our behalf. Jesus was not simply a "hired hand" who cared nothing for His sheep. His willingness to lay down His life demonstrates His love for us, His desire for us to live the lives God has envisioned for us, and His hope for us to live holy lives in communion with the Father.

"Why would Jesus choose to die on the cross?" is a question with which many Christians struggle at some point in their faith. We recognize the agony He must have endured. We recognize that He could have ended it at any point. And yet, He endured. Equally amazing is the fact that love motivated Jesus. Jesus loved us while we were still in our sin. Jesus loved us enough to endure the agony of the cross, both for the joy set before Him and also for His vision of what our lives could be like when we live in communion with God. Jesus determined that the high price He paid on the cross was worth it to see us redeemed and welcomed into God's family.

Respond

How has someone either been willing to or actually sacrificed for you in the past?

_____

_____

_____

_____

What is the biggest sacrifice you've ever made for someone else?

_____

_____

_____

_____

Could anything other than love have motivated Jesus to die on the cross on our behalf? Why or why not?

_____

_____

_____

_____

What is the relationship between Jesus's love for us and his vision for our lives as part of God's family?

_____

_____

_____

_____

Day 24
The Equipping Shepherd

Now may the God of peace who brought again from the dead our Lord Jesus, the great shepherd of the sheep, by the blood of the eternal covenant, equip you with everything good that you may do his will, working in us that which is pleasing in his sight, through Jesus Christ, to whom be glory forever and ever. Amen.

—Hebrews 13:20–21

My family didn't have a lot of extra resources when I was growing up. While I was able to play baseball and basketball, we simply didn't have the extra income for me to explore interests like guitar. Now, as a parent, I'm fortunate enough to both have some additional resources and to have family members who want to help our kids explore their interests. My wife and I want our kids to have every opportunity and all the resources and knowledge they need to be able to become whoever and whatever it is that God has shaped them to be.

Read Hebrews 13:20–21. God wants to equip you "with everything good." For what purpose? So that you can be happy? No. So that you can do His will. So that your life, your work, and your service is "pleasing in his sight." How does God equip us "with everything good"? By the power with which He raised Jesus from the dead and by the power of Jesus's shed blood that washes away our sin and pays the price of walking in a new life with God.

You may not feel like you have "everything good" that you need in order to accomplish God's will in your life, your family, your church, your work, or your community. But if you know Jesus, you have access to everything you need—a relationship with God and access to the power that raised Jesus from the dead. Like a loving parent who wants you to realize the best version of yourself, God *desires* for you to live in His grace and power to accomplish His will. When we live this way, we find this great truth: living to please God and accomplish His purposes over our own is the surest path to a joyful, happy life.

Jesus, the I AM

Respond

Was there a sport or activity that you wanted to do growing up that you were never able to do?

_____
_____
_____
_____

What kinds of "good" things does God equip us with to accomplish His will?

_____
_____
_____
_____

Why do you think so many Christians struggle with the idea of living to please God over themselves?

_____
_____
_____
_____

In what ways have you found joy and happiness in serving God's purposes over your own?

_____
_____
_____
_____

Day 25
The Sheep Know Him

My sheep hear my voice, and I know them, and they follow me.

—John 10:27

I'm an incredibly sound sleeper. In my life I've slept through a tornado that touched down a mile from my house, a bona fide California earthquake, and our home's alarm system going off for an hour and a half right outside my bedroom window along with the subsequent fire, police, and ambulance response. In spite of that, there's one thing that's guaranteed to rouse me from my deepest slumber: someone in my family saying my name. If my wife or one of my kids says my name, I'm immediately awake and ready to do whatever it is they need.

Read John 10:22–30. As Jesus was being questioned by the people about His identity, He remarked that they couldn't believe the works that He had performed because they were not among His sheep. Jesus's sheep not only recognized the works He performed but also knew His voice and responded to it by following Him. As a result, Jesus's sheep received eternal life and a place of security in the Father's hands. Satan himself wouldn't be able to snatch Jesus's sheep from their place in the Father's grasp. To tie a bow on these claims, Jesus stated that He was one with the Father.

What does Jesus's voice sound like to you? It's unlikely that you've ever heard an audible voice, so how do you discern whether that voice you hear belongs to Jesus or if it's simply your own fear? The criticisms of others? Satan? Focus on the content of the voice's message. While Jesus won't always affirm you and make you feel good about yourself, even His calls to repentance come from a place of love and care for His sheep. His desire for us, as His children, is always to give us abundant life through following Him more closely. Listen for how that voice is leading you to follow Jesus more intimately today.

Respond

Who has the most distinctive voice you know? What about it is distinctive?

_____

_____

_____

_____

When was the last time you felt like you heard Jesus's voice? What did He say? How did it "sound"?

_____

_____

_____

_____

How can we discern whether the voice we hear is truly Jesus's voice?

_____

_____

_____

_____

What habits or practices can help you to hear the voice of Jesus over all the noise of your life?

_____

_____

_____

_____

SECTION 6

I AM the Way, the Truth, and the Life

Benjie Shaw

Day 26
The Way, the Truth, and the Life

Jesus said to him, "I am the way, and the truth, and the life. No one comes to the Father except through me."

—John 14:6

Smartphones have completely eliminated the phenomenon of being lost. Gone are the days of receiving an address, studying an atlas, and hoping for the best. Nothing quite resembles the sudden realization that, while you thought you were on the correct road to your destination, you've actually traveled an hour and a half in the opposite direction. You may have even needed to confront a man's worst nightmare: asking a stranger for directions. Even then, these strangers were often not helpful. There was a good chance that the directions you received included instruction to "turn left at the old Smith barn," your helper not seeming to realize that you had no idea who the Smiths were, much less where their old barn was located.

Read John 14:1–6. Jesus knew that His crucifixion and death were soon coming. While He also knew He would be resurrected, Jesus knew the impact that seeing Him betrayed and killed would have on His disciples. So Jesus attempted to reassure them by letting them know that, when He left, He would be going to prepare a place for them. He reminded them that they knew the way to where He was going. Thomas asked a simple, but insightful question: "We don't even know where You're going, so how will we know how to get there?" Jesus's response was even more insightful. He informed His disciples that He, Himself, was the way, the truth, and the life, and that in following after Him they would also find the Father.

Do you feel unsure of what path to take? Follow Jesus. He is your way. Are you questioning something you've always believed or thought to be true? Look to Jesus. He is your truth. Are you feeling weighed down by cares and burdens in life? Look to Jesus. Find your life in Him. Jesus knew that His followers would walk difficult roads. His promise to be our way, our truth, and our life means that we can find direction, purpose, meaning, and, ultimately, the Father Himself in any and every circumstance through Jesus.

Jesus, the I AM

Respond

When was the last time you were really and truly lost? How did you feel?

_____

_____

_____

How do you think the disciples felt when Jesus told them He was going away? What clues might Thomas's question give us?

_____

_____

_____

Which of Jesus's three identities here—the way, the truth, or the life—do you find the easiest to accept and live in? Why do you think that is?

_____

_____

_____

Which of Jesus's three identities here—the way, the truth, or the life—do you find the most difficult to accept and live in? Why do you think that is?

_____

_____

_____

Day 27
Grace and Truth

And the Word became flesh and dwelt among us, and we have seen his glory, glory as of the only Son from the Father, full of grace and truth.

—John 1:14

I'm not a car guy, but even I find some car problems to be easily identifiable. A low or dead battery, a flat tire, especially one that's been punctured, or even leaky coolant are pretty easy for me to point out. Recently, I added alignment issues to my easily identifiable car troubles list. Once I knew what it was, it seemed obvious. For weeks, I had felt vibrations in the steering wheel getting worse, noticed that my wheel was slightly turned even though I was driving straight, and the dull squeal of my tires had become sharper. Fortunately, we caught the problem before it got worse and discovered it to be a pretty easy fix.

Read John 1:14–18. Jesus, who existed with God forever before creation, put on flesh and lived as a human. John witnessed the incredible seeming contradiction of an eternal, all-powerful being putting on human flesh and walking around on earth with people. How did John describe this phenomenon? John noted that Jesus was "full of grace and truth." In fact, the very reason Jesus was able to offer grace to people was because of His eternal nature. Moses gave the law, but Jesus gave grace and truth. Even though no one has seen God, Jesus has made God known in the way He displayed grace and truth.

Like cars, people can easily get out of balance. It's easy for us to key in on one of these two distinctives of Jesus's ministry and hold it hard and fast over the other. If we tend to understand following Jesus as a combative resistance against temptation and culture, we emphasize that Jesus is the truth. We equip ourselves with the best theological and apologetic arguments to demonstrate the truth of the Gospel over and against the claims of the world. In doing so, we sometimes demonize or mistreat others in the name of truth. If we tend to view Jesus as a call to care for the least of these and the oppressed, we emphasize Jesus's grace. We selflessly serve others and advocate for the poor, the downtrodden, and the oppressed in the name of grace. But sometimes we can find ourselves contradicting the truth Jesus proclaimed. The balance between grace and truth is tricky, but following Jesus wholeheartedly means walking in the tension of that balance as we follow Him.

Respond

What's one mechanical or structural problem that's easy for you to identify? Why is it so easy?

_____

_____

_____

_____

Do you think there is a tension between grace and truth? Why or why not?

_____

_____

_____

_____

What are the benefits of emphasizing truth? What are the potential pitfalls?

_____

_____

_____

_____

What are the benefits of emphasizing grace? What are the potential pitfalls?

_____

_____

_____

_____

Day 28
Truth Will Set You Free

You will know the truth, and the truth will set you free.

—John 8:32

Freedom from sin becomes a difficult concept the longer I follow Jesus. I understand it conceptually. Sometimes, I see dramatic instances of someone being set free from sin as they grow in their faith. But my life isn't characterized by any of what we classify as "big sins" from which to be delivered: I'm not an alcoholic, not addicted to pornography, I'm faithful to my wife, I'm truthful, I don't smoke or gamble. It's easy for me to lapse into thinking that Jesus's promise of being set free by the truth has already been fulfilled. "Good job, Jesus! You did it!"

Read John 8:31–36. Jesus connected the process of being freed from sin by truth to the act of abiding in His word. His listeners, reacting to the imagery of being enslaved, protested that they had never been slaves to anyone in their lives. As far as they knew, they were free. Once again, Jesus's audience missed the deeper meaning of His words. Jesus wasn't referring to physical slavery. He meant spiritual slavery. All sin leads to enslavement to even more sin. The only way out of the cycle is to be set free by someone who wasn't a slave: Jesus. When Jesus sets a person free, that person experiences true freedom.

In spite of the temptation to believe that I have "arrived" at a place of maturity where I no longer need Jesus's promise of freedom from sin, I, like everyone else, still have sin from which I need to be delivered. If all sin is sin, as we have often been told, then the pride I feel in my heart is just as toxic to my spirit as alcoholism. The jealousy I feel in my heart when someone else gets what I think I deserve is just as destructive to my spirit as pornography. Fortunately, Jesus can set us free from these as well. The key to deliverance is also the same: abide in His Word. When we allow our hearts and minds to be filled with the truth of Scripture against the lies of Satan that lead to our enslavement to sin, we will know the truth. Then, Jesus begins the work of liberating us and setting us free forever.

Respond

Why do you think we classify sin into "big" and "small" categories?

_____

_____

_____

_____

Are you ever tempted to think that your sin isn't as big of a deal because it isn't "big"?

_____

_____

_____

_____

How does knowing the truth about sin set us free?

_____

_____

_____

_____

How have you experienced the relationship between abiding in Jesus's truth and freedom from sin?

_____

_____

_____

_____

Day 29
Abundant Life

I came that they may have life and have it abundantly.

—John 10:10

et's play a quick game of word association. When you hear the word *life*, what do you think of? Being a recovering pessimist by nature, my associations aren't always the most positive. I think about work, chores, schedules, and obligations before I think about family, friends, and activities that I enjoy. Being a task-oriented person, I also tend to think more about the *whats* of life than the *qualities* of life. I understand that life is made up of a mixture of all these things in my head, but it can be difficult for that knowledge to work its way from my head to my heart.

Read John 10:10. Note that Jesus's declaration that He has come to give life abundantly to His followers is located between His claims to be both the door of the sheep and the good shepherd. As the door, Jesus is the only source of life. We can search for meaning, purpose, fulfillment, and a million other things in a million other places. But we will only find the answer to our deepest longings and questions in the person and work of Jesus. As the good shepherd, Jesus wants us to find those answers in abundance. He isn't looking to lead us to some sparse field where we get just enough sustenance to get by. No, Jesus wants us to experience all the best parts of life, through which we find ultimate fulfillment—in abundance—because He is good.

Abundant life in Jesus isn't something that we have to wait for until we die and go to heaven. Abundant life in Jesus is accessible right now to everyone who calls on His name. However, we live in this abundance on Jesus's terms. We don't get to decide that abundant life means getting that promotion or the fancy new car. Living in the abundant life Jesus desires for us means learning to live in His rhythms and patterns of life and finding ultimate satisfaction, peace, purpose, and meaning in Him.

Respond

What are the first four or five words that pop into your head when you read the word "life"?

_____

_____

_____

_____

How might those words influence your understanding of Jesus's desire for you to live an abundant life both positively and negatively?

_____

_____

_____

_____

Why is it important to understand that Jesus is the source of abundant life?

_____

_____

_____

_____

Do you feel like you are living in the abundant life Jesus desires for you? Why or why not?

_____

_____

_____

_____

Day 30
The Purpose of Truth

Then Pilate said to him, "So you are a king?" Jesus answered, "You say that I am a king. For this purpose I was born and for this purpose I have come into the world—to bear witness to the truth. Everyone who is of the truth listens to my voice."

—John 18:37

One of my favorite recent social media trends is the videos people make about crazy things they just learned that they feel like they should have known a long time ago. Usually titled "I was today years old when I learned . . .," these videos contain life hacks about cooking, cleaning, money management, and countless other subjects. Through these videos I learned that skillets themselves can be flipped, not just the contents in them. Grilled-cheese making has gotten much easier now that I know to lift the sandwich off of the skillet, flip the skillet on top of the sandwich, then flip the sandwich and skillet together easily back onto the surface of the stove. Knowing this has made my cooking experience easier.

Read John 18:33–38. The religious leaders brought Jesus before Pilate seeking Jesus's execution. Pilate pulled Jesus aside and interviewed Him privately. As the Roman governor, Pilate was only interested in discovering whether or not the charges the religious leaders brought against Jesus were true—was Jesus calling Himself a king? Jesus steered the topic away from the simple facts of the matter into a conversation about purpose and truth. Jesus noted that His kingdom was not of this world and that He existed to testify to the truth. Unable to hear Jesus's meaning, Pilate dismissively ended the conversation.

Jesus's entire life and ministry were meant to point people to the truth. Every aspect of Jesus's life and ministry testified to the truth—the truth about God, the truth about God's purposes, the truth about relationships, even the truth about those whom He came to earth for. Sometimes these truths can feel difficult to discern. More often, the truth is so plain and seemingly simple that we find reasons not to live by it. Like Pilate, we can find ourselves asking, "What is truth?" when the truth is simple obedience. Life works better when we live by the truth of Jesus, whether in the complicated or in the simple.

Respond

What is the best "life hack" that you've ever learned?

_____

_____

_____

_____

When have you missed the point of a conversation like Pilate did in this passage?

_____

_____

_____

_____

How does Jesus's life testify to the truth?

_____

_____

_____

_____

Do you find it easier to live in Jesus's truth in big or small things? Why do you think that is?

_____

_____

_____

_____

SECTION 7

I AM the True Vine

Benjie Shaw

Day 31
The True Vine

I am the true vine, and my Father is the vinedresser.

—John 15:1

Home ownership has taught me a lot of lessons in a trial-by-fire format. One particularly painful lesson involved my first experience with poison ivy. After getting the first case of poison ivy I ever had in my life (and it was bad), I learned that I had to be vigilant every spring and summer to identify the vine as it infiltrated my yard. If I failed to do this, the vine would spread throughout an entire area, making it more likely that I would have another itchy experience. I also discovered that the whole process could be eliminated if I could identify the source of the vine and remove it. While difficult to do, this was the surest bet to control my poison ivy problem.

Read John 15:1–2. As Jesus prepared His disciples for His betrayal and death, He led them on a walk to the Garden of Gethsemane to pray. The conversation they had is recorded in detail in the Gospel of John and contains some of the most personal instructions from Jesus to His followers recorded in any of the Gospels. Among the wisdom Jesus shared with them was the truth that Jesus Himself was the vine by which His followers would be connected to God. As they remained connected to Jesus, they would bear fruit. God would orchestrate their lives so that they bore more and more fruit and they remained connected to Jesus.

The vine to which we are connected dictates the type of "fruit" we produce. Poison ivy vines produce an uncomfortable, harmful result on a person's body. But staying connected to Jesus produces desirable fruit in our minds, hearts, relationships, and souls. We are able to stay connected to the Father by staying connected to the vine that is Jesus through reading, studying, and reflecting on His Word, through prayer, through community with other believers, through serving others, and other spiritual disciplines. The old saying is true: if you feel distant from God, it's not God that has moved.

Respond

Like the poison ivy in my yard, what is something that snuck into your life and took a lot of work to uproot?

_____

_____

_____

_____

How is Jesus the vine?

_____

_____

_____

_____

What practices or habits are in your life to help you stay connected to Jesus?

_____

_____

_____

_____

What habits or practices do you need to take up to help you stay connected to Jesus?

_____

_____

_____

_____

Day 32
The Fruit of the Spirit

But the fruit of the Spirit is love, joy, peace, patience, kindness, goodness, faithfulness, gentleness, self-control; against such things there is no law.

—Galatians 5:22–23

I'm oddly intrigued by survival TV shows. You know the kind I mean. The kind where one person or a group of people get left out in the wild with minimal provisions. They are expected to survive for a certain amount of time or make it to a specific checkpoint. Eventually, the participants wind up foraging for food of some kind. They comb through what oftentimes look like regular bushes to me and can easily tell the difference between fruit that is safe to eat and fruit that is poisonous. They're able to make that distinction easily because they've spent time studying the signs of fruit that nourishes life and the fruit that can end or hinder it.

Read Galatians 5:22–23. Jesus is the vine from which God wants to produce fruit in our lives. Thankfully, this passage spells out specific characteristics that God is looking to grow in our lives from our connection with Jesus. These are the traits and characteristics that, enabled by the Holy Spirit, lead to life that flourishes in Him. If a characteristic or trait isn't on this list, it is likely that it doesn't lead to our flourishing as Christians. God, in His wisdom, has given us tremendous detail about the fruit that leads to life.

Christians can spend a lot of time talking about growing spiritually without any real idea of what that means outside of doing things—a devotional time, attending church, giving, serving. But none of those external measurements of maturity give us a window into our hearts and souls. Jesus regularly critiqued people who met these external measurements but whose hearts and souls were in poor spiritual condition. Instead of only weighing maturity against external measurements, we would also do well to measure our lives against the fruit of the Spirit.

Respond

Do you tend to think of spiritual maturity by external behavior or internal attitudes? Why?

_____

_____

_____

_____

Do you think it's possible to have all the external markers of spiritual maturity but lack the fruit of the Spirit? Why or why not?

_____

_____

_____

_____

Why is it important to know the kind of fruit Jesus wants to produce in our lives?

_____

_____

_____

_____

Which of the fruit of the Spirit is the most difficult for you? Can you think of a way to intentionally cultivate that fruit in your life?

_____

_____

_____

_____

Day 33
Abide in Me

I am the vine; you are the branches. Whoever abides in me and I in him, he it is that bears much fruit, for apart from me you can do nothing."

—John 15:5

I've always been a pretty independent person. Since I was a teenager, I've made most of my own decisions. That worked fine when my decisions mostly impacted only me. That all changed when I married my wife. Suddenly, my decisions didn't just immediately impact me alone anymore. Shifting from a "me" to a "we" thinking process was a struggle for me. I knew I was married and I loved my wife, but for a time I had to slow down my decision-making process to remind myself that my choices impacted more than myself. Thankfully, I learned this lesson and it's no longer a struggle. But I wouldn't have arrived at this place without that intentional process of reminding myself of my new situation.

Read John 15:4–7. As Jesus prepared His disciples for His forthcoming betrayal and death, He exhorted them to abide in Him. He plainly instructed them that they would not be fruitful in the life and task that Jesus had set before them if they failed to abide in Him. If they were faithful in abiding, fruit would come just as it did on the branch of a healthy vine. As they lived in this posture of abiding in Jesus, the disciples could ask whatever they wanted from the Father in prayer and God would give it to them because they would find that they wanted what Jesus wanted.

Abiding takes work. In our digital age, millions of things can distract us from the work of abiding in Christ. As a newlywed, I had to slow down and intentionally think through decisions in a new way. We Christians also benefit from slowing down our routines and evaluating them through the lens of abiding in Christ. More is at stake in this process than an optional next level of spiritual maturity. Your fruitfulness as a follower of Christ is at stake.

Respond

What is one way of thinking that was more difficult to unlearn than you anticipated?

_____

_____

_____

_____

Why is being fruitful in our faith tied to our ability to abide in Christ?

_____

_____

_____

_____

What things in your life might distract you from abiding in Christ?

_____

_____

_____

_____

Outside of a consistent devotional life, what habits or practices can we establish to help us abide in Christ throughout the day?

_____

_____

_____

_____

Day 34
Glorify God

By this my Father is glorified, that you bear much fruit and so prove to be my disciples. As the Father has loved me, so have I loved you. Abide in my love.

—John 15:8–9

I don't know where *that* comes from!" That's a remark my wife and I will sarcastically make to one another when one of our kids does or says something that they obviously learned from or inherited from one of us. Sometimes flattering, sometimes embarrassing, there are moments when our kids demonstrate that they are ours beyond a shadow of a reasonable doubt. My daughter is an early riser, like me. My son loves to cuddle and take naps like my wife. My daughter loves to read and has my sense of humor. My son has his mother's empathy for others.

Read John 15:8–11. When followers of Jesus bear spiritual fruit, God is glorified. It is this spiritual fruit that proves that we belong to Jesus. But spiritual fruit isn't produced out of our own human will. No, it is only produced through learning to live and abide in the love of God in Christ. Obedience to Christ, the part of the equation that is mostly up to us, is how we demonstrate our love for Him. However, this obedience isn't meant to be done out of obligation. Instead, we find that we experience great joy when we live in obedience to Jesus. His joy fills our hearts and lives, which, in turn, glorifies God.

We begin to think, act, and talk like those whom we are around the most. Just like my kids pick up on both my and my wife's personalities, vocabulary, and actions, followers of Jesus are influenced by Jesus as we strive to abide in Him. Far from just a sentimental attachment, Jesus desires our obedience to Him—not because He is a cosmic dictator who wants authority over our lives, but because He knows that we will find inexhaustible joy in obedience to Him. We experience His love regularly, and that impacts how we interact with others. We will bear much spiritual fruit and glorify God with our lives as we live in obedience to Jesus.

Respond

What is one habit or trait that you picked up from your parents or another significant figure in your life?

_____

_____

_____

_____

Why is spiritual fruit not produced by human will?

_____

_____

_____

_____

What words do you think most people associate with joy?

_____

_____

_____

_____

Do you associate joy with obedience? Why or why not?

_____

_____

_____

_____

Day 35
Bear Fruit

You did not choose me, but I chose you and appointed you that you should go and bear fruit and that your fruit should abide, so that whatever you ask the Father in my name, he may give it to you.

—John 15:16

A few years ago, I became convicted about the lack of joy in my life. Even though I had a consistent devotional life, I wasn't experiencing the fruit of joy in following Jesus. I decided one of the ways that I could cultivate joy in my heart was to change the way I answered, "How are you?"—a question I heard variations of every day. Instead of focusing on items on my to-do list or something that was going on that was causing me stress, I determined to answer the question with something that was going well. Several months later, as I expressed that I was generally a pessimistic person to a new acquaintance, he responded with shock. "You're one of the happiest people I know," he said. He had met me after I made that one seemingly insignificant change in my life.

Read John 15:16–17. Jesus wants us to bear fruit. It's one of the reasons that He has chosen us as His followers. But Jesus doesn't want that fruit to be through the temporary exercise of our own will. The fruit that Jesus desires for us is fruit that abides—that is a true characteristic of our lives. As the fruit of following Jesus grows in our lives, we will find our will more conformed to His. And our requests of God become more in alignment with His will for our lives.

By our own power, we can decide to think, act, or respond in a way that is consistent with bearing fruit as a follower of Jesus a few times. But we must maintain a strong connection to Jesus, our vine, for our lives to characterize the fruit of following Jesus. Once that connection is established, seemingly small, even insignificant, changes can make a big difference in the fruit that is evidenced by our lives.

Respond

How is your connection with Jesus, your vine?

_____

_____

_____

_____

What habits or practices in your life help you maintain a personal connection with Jesus as your vine?

_____

_____

_____

_____

How is bearing fruit from the exercise of our will different from allowing it to come from a connection with Jesus?

_____

_____

_____

_____

Why do you think Jesus is concerned that the fruit of following Him abides in our lives?

_____

_____

_____

_____

SECTION 8

I AM the Resurrection and the Life

Benjie Shaw

Day 36
The Resurrection and the Life

Jesus said to her, "I am the resurrection and the life. Whoever believes in me, though he die, yet shall he live, and everyone who lives and believes in me shall never die. Do you believe this?"

—John 11:25–26

I asked my wife in shock, "Wait, he what?" She had just let me know that a friend with whom I had worked and attended seminary had died from brain cancer the day before. We had known he had cancer, but the last report we received suggested good news. While death rarely comes as welcome news, I was shocked that this friend in his mid-thirties, with whom I had worked and studied less than five years ago, had passed away. It took a few days to fully absorb the news, but the seeming finality of his death hit me as I was running errands one day. I wouldn't see this friend again on this side of eternity, but his story was just beginning.

Read John 11:17–27. Jesus knew the pain of the loss of a friend. When Jesus's good friend Lazarus died, Lazarus' sister Martha knew that Jesus could have prevented her brother's death. But Jesus did not arrive until two days after Lazarus's body was laid in his tomb. As Martha shared her grief with Jesus, Jesus declared that Lazarus would rise again. Most Jews believed in the ultimate resurrection of the righteous, so Martha easily agreed. She thought Jesus meant Lazarus would rise on the judgment day. But Jesus had something else in mind. He noted that those who believe in Him would live even though they may die because Jesus was the resurrection and the life.

Death is not the end for Christians. My friend now lives a more glorious existence than we can fathom because of his faith in Jesus. We know that Jesus sometimes heals us or people we care about when we face physical illness. We also know that sometimes He doesn't. Death eventually comes for all of us. For Christians, death is just the beginning to a glorious eternity filled with the fullness of life Jesus promised his followers. We can trust Him in this.

Respond

Have you been surprised by a friend or loved one's death? How did it make you feel?

_____

_____

_____

_____

Do you think most people are afraid of death? Why or why not?

_____

_____

_____

_____

How can Jesus's promise of resurrection and life comfort or challenge your thoughts about death?

_____

_____

_____

_____

How can knowing someone who died knew Jesus change the way we mourn his or her loss?

_____

_____

_____

_____

Day 37
He Has Borne Our Griefs

But he was pierced for our transgressions;
    he was crushed for our iniquities;
upon him was the chastisement that brought us peace,
    and with his wounds we are healed.

—Isaiah 53:5

As a parent, watching you child experience hurt, pain, and sadness is heartbreaking. My children are both very small, so what qualifies as "heartbreaking" for them is relatively minor. But seeing the tears well up in their eyes and their cheeks slowly turn red as the sobs start coming has a way of melting my heart. I know that as they grow and their heartbreaks become more heartbreaking, my experience of hurt on their behalf is likely to grow. I've witnessed my own parents' and in-laws' hearts break as my wife and I have shared our more "adult" heartbreaks with them over the years. Loving someone involves feeling his or her pain in very real ways as if it were happening to you.

Read Isaiah 53:4–6. Even though Jesus took on the pain of others, people didn't recognize that as a loving act. But that reality didn't stop Jesus from following through with His mission to take on our sin and heal us through the pain and rejection that He experienced on the cross. We are wandering sheep. God's plan from the beginning of time has always been to bring His sheep back through the loving sacrifice of His son.

I love my children more than I can express. Yet, I cannot begin to imagine the depth of love that Jesus felt for all people that motivated Him to take on their sorrows, still be rejected by most of them, and yet persist in giving His life on the cross to pay the price for sin. We tend to emphasize Jesus's love in connection with His willingness to die on our behalf. But we also must acknowledge that His love is demonstrated in His willingness to walk with us through our pain and sorrow.

Respond

When have you experienced heartbreak as you watched someone you love struggle?

_____

_____

_____

_____

Why do you think people fail to see Jesus taking on their griefs as a loving act?

_____

_____

_____

_____

How have you experienced Jesus's love as He walked with you through sorrow?

_____

_____

_____

_____

Are you currently facing any sorrows or struggles that you are trying to face on your own? How can Jesus bear your griefs today?

_____

_____

_____

_____

Day 38
The Work of Redemption

And because of him you are in Christ Jesus, who became to us wisdom from God, righteousness and sanctification and redemption.

—1 Corinthians 1:30

I didn't always get along with one of my supervisors. As a result, serving alongside him could be difficult because we were rarely on the same page. Finding common ground would get tricky, but then something unexpected would happen. I would overhear a conversation he had with a student seeking advice. When I expected him to say something a little out there that I might have to attempt to soften later with the student, he was compassionate. Understanding. Caring. Empathetic. Qualities that, at times, I wondered if he had. I realized that, despite my impressions of him, there was more to this somewhat difficult man than met the eye.

Read 1 Corinthians 1:26–30. God has a habit of using people or things in the world that appear to be "low" to do His work. The same is true in the church. Many within the church do not have the qualifications we might prefer for someone to be entrusted with the task of growing God's kingdom on earth as it is in heaven. But God has chosen them (and you!) for this very purpose. God's desire is that we find in Jesus all that we need in life. In fact, Jesus has provided all that we need to live the life that God desires for us. There is more to knowing and following Jesus than what we tend to be content with.

Like a well that will never run dry or a mine whose riches are inexhaustible, so is following Jesus. The riches and depths of His wisdom, righteousness, sanctification, and redemption will surprise us for our entire lives as we know Him more intimately. This reality ought to inspire us to worship Jesus. Draw nearer to the One who will continually surprise but never disappoint us.

Jesus, the I AM

Respond

Describe a time when someone's behavior surprised you in a good way.

_____

_____

_____

_____

Why do you think God chooses "low" and "weak" things and people to accomplish His purposes?

_____

_____

_____

_____

Do you think it is tempting for people to live as if they know all there is to know about what Jesus has done for us? Why or why not?

_____

_____

_____

_____

How can the knowledge that the riches of knowing Jesus are inexhaustible lead us to worship Him?

_____

_____

_____

_____

Day 39
Resurrection and Newness

We were buried therefore with him by baptism into death, in order that, just as Christ was raised from the dead by the glory of the Father, we too might walk in newness of life. For if we have been united with him in a death like his, we shall certainly be united with him in a resurrection like his.

—Romans 6:4–5

I was 14 when I confessed my sins and trusted Christ as my Savior. I was a "good" kid so I don't have one of those dramatic conversion stories about how, after I trusted Jesus, I stopped doing drugs or sleeping around or partying or anything like that. From a behavior standpoint, my conversion probably looked a little unremarkable. But the one thing I distinctly remember from that day was the ride home. We lived in a rural valley with small mountains lining either side of the road from the church to our house. As we made the drive we had made literally hundreds of times before, I took it all in, feeling as if I were seeing it for the first time.

Read Romans 6:4–5. When Christians make the decision to follow Christ and are baptized, we are depicting a stunning spiritual reality. The waters come over us as a picture of both Jesus's death and of our death to our old lives. As the waters recede, we model both Jesus's resurrection and the new life that He brings to us. The entire scene is meant to be a physical depiction of the spiritual work God has done in our lives.

While the outer circumstances of our conversion may appear to be more or less dramatic than others, the inner circumstances of everyone's conversion are just as stunning. We have passed from spiritual death to spiritual life through the work of Jesus! He has raised us from spiritual death to walk in eternal life with Him beginning at the moment you made your profession of faith! We are united with Christ and have access to a new kind of life empowered by the Holy Spirit. Praise God!

Jesus, the I AM

Respond

What was your life like before you came to faith in Christ?

_____

_____

_____

_____

Do you struggle with comparing your testimony to others? Why or why not?

_____

_____

_____

_____

Regardless of the external circumstances of anyone's testimony, what are the spiritual realities we all experienced before we came to know Christ?

_____

_____

_____

_____

Is it important for us to regularly remind ourselves of the spiritual transformation we experienced in Christ? If so, how can we do that?

_____

_____

_____

_____

Day 40
He Is Risen!

He is not here, for he has risen, as he said. Come, see the place where he lay.

—Matthew 28:6

I remember the moment I knew I was going to marry my wife. We had not been dating for long. It wasn't a magical moment with all the accompanying romantic bells and whistles. We were just having a conversation in her dorm room when this overwhelming impression hit me that my life was about to be different because God had brought this girl into my life. It was something I had never felt before and something I wasn't entirely sure what to do with. In that moment, there was no escaping the thought that my life was about to be different.

Read Matthew 28:1–10. Mary Magdalene and the other Mary had to be completely unprepared for the scene they witnessed at the tomb. Likely expecting to pay a quick visit to the place where Jesus lay, they instead found Roman soldiers looking "like dead men," the stone rolled away, and an angel with a message for them sitting on the stone. The two Marys were the first to hear the good news that Jesus had been raised. They were also the first charged with the task of telling others this good news. As if that weren't enough, they were also the first to see and speak to the resurrected Christ. Life had changed for the two Marys.

Despite the predictions of the prophets and Jesus's own predictions, His resurrection was unexpected to His followers. The agenda of the two Marys for their Sunday morning stroll did not include having an experience with the resurrected Christ. It's easy for us to wonder why His followers didn't just "get it" because it seems so obvious to us. And yet, how often are we surprised when Jesus shows up in places or in people that we didn't expect? Easter is the proclamation of the expected yet surprising work of Jesus. He is risen. And life will never be the same.

Respond

What is one moment in which you knew life would be different going forward?

_____

_____

_____

_____

What do you think the two Marys felt as they arrived at the tomb? When they saw it was empty?

_____

_____

_____

_____

How has Jesus surprised you by showing up in places or people you didn't expect Him?

_____

_____

_____

_____

How can worshipping Jesus this Easter be both expected and surprising?

_____

_____

_____

_____

About the Authors

Margie Williamson accepted Christ as her Savior and Lord on Easter Sunday 1959 and was baptized the same evening. She discovered early a desire to write and has been working on that since she was a child. She has written devotionals, Bible study curriculum, articles, and stories. Margie now works as Faith Editor and Feature Writer for NowHabersham.com and loves the opportunity to discover stories about the North Georgia mountains and the people who live there. After years of full-time ministry, Margie and husband Bob have retired to the mountains and wake up every morning aware of all the blessings God has bestowed upon them.

Benjie Shaw is a campus minister in the metro Memphis area through the Tennessee Baptist Mission Board. He is married to Jenna, dad to Ava and Caleb, has a horse-sized puppy, is a self-described coffee snob, and Marvel nerd. When he's not chasing his kids around, he can be found in his garage gym or daydreaming about mountains. You can connect with Benjie's blog and ministry at his website: www.benjieshaw.com.

Printed in the USA
CPSIA information can be obtained
at www.ICGtesting.com
LVHW020410251123
764788LV00007B/681

9 781632 041241